To: Elijah

With Love Edwina L. Le

God Loves You!

Thank You God for My Food

Edwina Grice Neely

Illustrated by Linda Grice Lynch

ISBN: 1-4392-6063-X
ISBN-13: 9781439260630

To order additional copies, visit www.booksurge.com or contact the author directly at edwinaneely@comcast.net. More contact information is on page 31.

This book was:
Edited by Priska Neely
Designed by Nicole Neely
Cover Art and Illustrations by Linda Grice Lynch

Printed in U.S.A.

Neely, Edwina Grice
    Thank You God for My Food.

God loves us all the same
and He knows us all by name.

My name is

_____

*"You should be happy because your
names are written in heaven."*
Luke10:20, ICB

DEDICATED TO:

God, the maker of our food, who put it in my mind to write this book.

Isaiah, my grandson, who gave me the excitement to complete it.

Dear Parents,

Some of the first words our children utter are about food. It is exciting to have a book that teaches the names of everyday foods, explains how they can be prepared, and draws a Biblical connection.

I have been a teacher for over thirty years and have encountered so many children who are in the dark about the origins of food. I once asked a kindergartener, "Where do raisins come from?" His response: "The grocery store." In this book, children will learn about things that we often take for granted. Raisins come from grapes, bread is made with flour from wheat, and honey is made by special bees.

It will be exciting to watch your child become familiar with these foods and gain enhanced reading skills. This book will teach your child to sight-read the names. With the colorful illustrations and catchy rhymes, you will be surprised at how quickly your child will learn fun facts about the food they love. Be sure to check out the "activity go-alongs" in the back of the book to extend the experience.

Food is truly a gift from God. Children will learn to be thankful for the delicious food God has made. To hear them say, "*Thank you God for my food*," is a sweet sound to my ears.

Blessings,
Edwina Neely

Food

[Paste a drawing or picture of your favorite food here.]

"He (God) gives **food** to every living creature."

Psalm 136:25, ICB

**Thank You God
for food to eat.
All this food!
It's such a treat.**

Apples

"...refresh me with **apples**..."

Song of Solomon 2:5, ICB

**Thank You God
for apples. Why?
I just love my
Mommy's pie.**

Grapes

"...you may eat as many **grapes** as you wish..."

Deuteronomy 23:24, ICB

**Thank You God
for grapes to munch--
crunchy, juicy,
all in a bunch.**

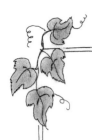

Raisins

" ...she took... cakes
of **raisins**."

I Samuel 25:18, ICB

**Thank You God
for raisins to chew.
Dried up grapes
make something new.**

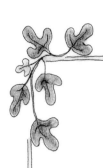

Figs

"There are young figs on the fig trees."

Song of Solomon 2:13, ICB

**Thank You God
for fig bars too.
They come from
figs made by you.**

Wheat

" I would give you the
finest **wheat**."

Psalm 81:16, ICB

**Thank You God for
wheat to make
bread, cookies,
and yummy cake.**

Honey

"My child, eat honey
because it is good."

Proverbs 24:13, ICB

**Thank You God
for sweet** honey**,
made by the
buzzing honeybee.**

Olives

**"You will have olive trees
in all your land."**

Deuteronomy 28:40, ICB

**Thank You God
for olives to snack.
I like the green
and love the black.**

Nuts

"I went down into the orchard of **nut** trees."

Song of Solomon 6:11, ICB

**Thank You God
for nuts on trees.
Mmm mmm.
May I have more please?**

Milk

"…He also gave them…milk."

Genesis 18:8, ICB

**Thank You God
for milk to enjoy,
from cows, rice,
almonds and soy.**

**Strong and healthy
I will be
eating food God
made for me.**

Now I pray,
to God I say,
"Thank you God for my food."

Thank You God For My Food

Thank you God for food to eat.
All this food! It's such a treat.

Thank you God for apples. Why?
I just love my Mommy's pie.

Thank You God for grapes to munch--
crunchy, juicy, all in a bunch.

Thank you God for raisins to chew.
Dried up grapes make something new.

Thank You God for fig bars too.
They come from figs made by you.

Thank You God for wheat to make
bread, cookies, and yummy cake.

Thank you God for sweet honey,
made by the buzzing honeybee.

Thank You God for olives to snack.
I like the green and love the black.

Thank You God for nuts on trees.
Mmm mmm. May I have more please?

Thank You God for milk to enjoy,
from cows, rice, almonds and soy.

Strong and healthy I will be,
eating food God made for me.

Now I pray, to God I say,
"Thank You, God for my food".

"Activity Go-Alongs"

I have included an activity to go along with each food highlighted in the book. May you and your child enjoy the many different types of food God has made to keep us happy and healthy.

Apple

Sugarless Apple Pie
- 6 medium apples (McIntosh are my favorite)
- Small can of frozen unsweetened apple juice
- 2 tablespoons flour
- Butter (Optional)
- Spices (cinnamon/nutmeg)
- Pastry for a double crust pie

Mix all ingredients, except the butter, in a bowl. Pour mixture into a pastry-lined 9" pie pan and dot with butter. Place top crust on and cut in slits, seal and flute the edges. Bake @ 350 degrees until apples are done and crust is golden brown.

Explorations
- Slice an apple across and discover the star in the middle.
- Get red, green, and yellow apples. Have your child taste them and choose a favorite.

Grapes

Grape Juice
Put 2 cups of concord grapes in a double boiler. Boil grapes until juice oozes out. Drain the juice off of the grapes. Chill juice. Enjoy a nice glass of fresh juice. If the juice is too strong, dilute it with water. If your grapes aren't very sweet, sweeten to your taste with maple syrup or sugar.

You can use the leftover grapes to make a topping for toast or pancakes. Mash the leftover grapes to get the pulp out and strain. The thick juice can be sweetened as you like.

Raisins

"Ants on a log"
Cut strips of celery, fill with peanut butter and place a row of raisins on top. If peanut allergies are an issue, substitute the filling with cream cheese or any nut butter you like.

Figs

Compare the taste of fresh figs and dry figs.

Crush fresh figs in a blender with a small apple, pineapple juice, or water until it gets to a spreadable texture. Use the fig spread on toast or crackers.

Wheat

Honey Wheat Yeast Biscuits
- 1 1/3 cup warm water
- 1 package yeast
- 2 cups whole wheat flour
- 2 cups unbleached white flour
- 1 teaspoon salt
- 2 Tablespoons honey
- 1/4 cup canola oil (or any vegetable oil)

Mix all ingredients. Oil hands and shape dough into biscuits. Children like to shape the dough into balls, worms, bears, turtles, and other creative creatures. Put in greased pans, cover, and let rise for 20 minutes. If you want the texture to resemble buns instead of biscuits let it rise until it doubles in size. Bake at 400 degrees for 20-30 minutes.

Get a stalk of real wheat from a florist or nearby farm to show where wheat flour originates.

Honey

Explorations
Get honey with the honeycomb inside. Taste it. Have it on some bread.
Visit a Nature Center where you can see a beehive in action.

Olives

Taste Test
Get a variety of olives, pitted, sun ripened, green and black, and compare the taste.

Nuts

Mix and Match
Get nuts in the shell and the same nuts out of the shell (raw). See if your child can match the shelled and unshelled nuts.

*Be very sure you child is old enough to eat nuts!

Milk

Fruit Smoothie
(The following is good with almond milk.)

1 cup frozen fruit (strawberries, pineapple, blueberries, etc)
1 cup milk (any kind you like)

Blend for one minute. Sweeten to taste. This recipe serves 1-2 people.

I hope you have enjoyed this book.

Let us be thankful for great food and our awesome God.

Author's Contact Information
Edwina Neely • 1305 Mimosa Lane • Silver Spring, MD 20904
301.384.3505 • edwinaneely@comcast.net

4351274

Made in the USA
Charleston, SC
07 January 2010